Detective Tilak

Written by Julia Jarman
Illustrated by Julie Park

Chapter 1

It was Monday morning and Sam and Rosie had just arrived at school. Mrs Hall was in the classroom and so was Mr Evans, the caretaker. They were looking at an empty table. They both looked very worried.

'The new computer has gone,' said Mrs Hall.
'Where has it gone?' asked Sam.
'We don't know,' said Mrs Hall.
'We think someone has stolen it,' said Mr Evans.

Tilak and Mo arrived. Then Carlo came into the classroom. Rosie told them all about the computer.

'We think someone has stolen it,' she said. Tilak went and spoke to Mrs Hall.

'How did the burglars get in?' he asked.

'I don't know,' she said.

'Were the doors locked?'
asked Tilak.
  'Yes,' said Mrs Hall.

'Was a window broken?'
asked Tilak.
  'No,' said Mrs Hall.

'Were the windows locked?'
asked Tilak.
  'I don't know,' said Mrs Hall.
She did look upset.

'Let's look at the windows,' said Tilak.

Sam told the others that Mrs Hall had called the police. 'They'll be here soon,' he said.

Everybody was upset about the computer.
'It's not fair,' said Mo.
'No, it's not fair,' said Rosie. 'Computers cost a lot of money.' Then she said to Carlo, 'Maybe your dad can magic it back.'

But Tilak said, 'We don't need a magician.
We need a detective.'
 'Oh yes!' laughed Mo.
'Detective Tilak!'
Then Rosie pointed out
of the window.

'Here are the police!' she said
as a police car came into the
playground. A policewoman
got out.

Chapter 2

The policewoman's name was PC Sharp.
Mrs Hall told her what had happened.

PC Sharp had a good
look round the school.

She talked to the other
teachers and she made
a lot of notes.

Then she looked at
all the doors and
all the windows.

'What about that little window?' said Tilak.
He was pointing to a little window at the side.
'That window's open,' he said.
  'It's very small,' said PC Sharp. 'I don't think anybody could get through there.'
  'A very small person could,' said Tilak.

Then Tilak saw something else.
In the mud under the window,
he saw some footprints.
He pointed them out to PC Sharp.
  'Somebody has been
walking about there,' he said.
'Look at the footprints.'

'They must be yours,' said PC Sharp.
'They're very small.'

Tilak looked at the
footprints. Then he looked
at his shoes.

'They're not mine,' he said.
'They don't match. My shoes
have got circles on them.'
  PC Sharp laughed and
said, 'You're right,
Detective Tilak!'

  She bent down and
looked at the footprints in
the mud. They were small
and narrow, and they had
wavy lines on them.

'You'd better look at all our shoes,' said Tilak.
'Good idea,' said PC Sharp, and she told
everybody to sit down so that she could look
at their shoes.

None of them matched the footprints
in the mud. 'We've got to find the shoes
which match,' said Tilak. 'Then we might know
who took the computer.'

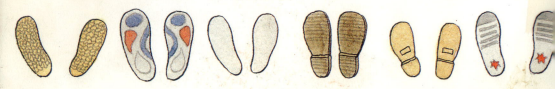

He thought for a moment, then he asked,
'Are there any fingerprints?'

PC Sharp looked at the window-ledge.

'I think so,' she said.

She took some powder from her bag and sprinkled it on the window-ledge. Then she got some sticky tape and put it on the powder. Finally, she pressed the tape onto some paper.

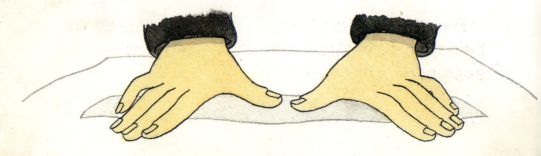

She held up the paper. 'Look,' she said. Everybody looked – and they saw black fingerprints on the white paper.

'They're small too,' said PC Sharp. 'They could belong to somebody here. So I'd better take everybody's fingerprints.'

They all went back into the classroom.
'Don't be worried,' said PC Sharp. 'I don't really think any of you stole the computer.'

One by one, they put their fingers onto an inky pad.

One by one, they made black fingerprints on the white paper.

PC Sharp looked carefully at all of the fingerprints. None of them matched the ones on the small window-ledge.

'We must find the ones which match,' said Tilak, 'Then we'll know who took the computer.'

'That's right,' said PC Sharp. 'You really would make a good detective.'

Everybody wanted the computer back.
Everybody wanted the police to catch the burglar.
'We'll do our best,' said PC Sharp.
But the days passed, and the police didn't
catch the burglar.

Chapter 3

Tilak thought about what PC Sharp had said to him. He wanted to be a detective and he wanted to help the police.

Every day, he looked at people's shoes.
'I wish you could find the burglar, Detective Tilak,' said Mr Evans.

Everybody called Tilak, 'Detective Tilak,' now. He had a magnifying glass and some binoculars— and some disguises!

A few days later,
Mo was going home with
Tilak. 'Let's both be
detectives,' said Mo and
she put on a moustache.
'Let's both look for the
burglar.'

Tilak put on a
moustache too – and a
pair of glasses. 'We are
looking for someone
very thin,' he said.
'Only someone thin
could get through
that little window.'

All the way home they looked for thin people. They saw an old lady who was very thin.

'I don't think Miss Link is a burglar,' laughed Tilak's mum. 'She's going to the shops.'

They saw a very
thin black cat.
  'It could be a cat
burglar,' laughed Mo.

  But Tilak didn't laugh. 'Look over
there,' he whispered. He was looking at two men
sitting outside the pub.

'That man's very thin,'
said Mo. 'And he's small.'

'What are they doing?'
said Tilak. 'They're sitting
outside the pub, but they
haven't got any drinks.'
'Maybe they're waiting
for someone,' said Mo.

'No,' said Tilak.
'I don't think so.
They're looking at
those houses. They're
looking at Miss Link's house.'

Tilak looked at the men
through his binoculars.
He looked carefully at the
thin man's shoes.

'I think he's the burglar,'
he said, giving his
binoculars to Mo.
'Look at the wavy lines
on his shoes.'

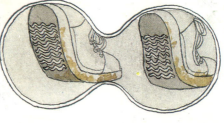

As Mo looked, the men
got up and walked towards
Miss Link's house.

Suddenly, the thin man climbed onto the wall.
'He's going into Miss Link's garden,' said Tilak.
'Quick,' said Mo. 'We must tell your mum.'

They ran back to Tilak's mum, waving their arms.
'Quick!' hissed Tilak, 'There's a burglar and
he's going to break into Miss Link's house.
I think he's the burglar who took our computer.
Come and look.'
Tilak's mum crept back with them.

They all hid behind a wall and watched the thin man trying to break in. He quickly opened a little window.

'He's climbing in,' hissed Tilak. 'Call the police, Mum!' Tilak's mum called 999 on her mobile phone.

'I want the police,' she said quietly. 'There's a burglary at 3, Maple Close. Come quickly and you can catch the burglar.'

The police did come quickly.
They came zooming
along in a police car and
PC Sharp was with them.

Two policemen caught the
burglars and took them off
to the police station.

PC Sharp stayed and
talked to Tilak. 'Well done,
Detective Tilak,' she said.

Next day, PC Sharp came to school and told the class what had happened. The police had taken the men's fingerprints and the thin man's had matched the ones on the window-ledge at school.

Everybody cheered, and there was a specially big cheer for Detective Tilak!

Then PC Sharp went out to her car and she came back with their computer!